KEEPING SAFE

WITH
FRIENDS AND FAMILY

by Honor Head

W
FRANKLIN WATTS
LONDON • SYDNEY

First published in 2014 by Franklin Watts

Copyright © Arcturus Holdings Limited

Franklin Watts
338 Euston Road
London NW1 3BH
Franklin Watts Australia
Level 17/207 Kent Street, Sydney NSW 2000

Produced by Arcturus Holdings Limited,
26/27 Bickels Yard, 151–153 Bermondsey Street, London SE1 3HA

Editors: Penny Worms and Joe Harris
Designer: Emma Randall
Cover designer: Emma Randall
Original design concept: Elaine Wilkinson

Picture credits: All images courtesy of Shutterstock.

A CIP catalogue record for this book is available from the British Library.

Dewey Decimal Classification Number 613.6

ISBN 978 1 4451 3251 8

Printed in China

Franklin Watts is a division of Hachette Children's Books,
an Hachette UK company.

www.hachette.co.uk

SL004068UK
Supplier 03, Date 0614, Print Run 3441

CONTENTS

MAKING DECISIONS

As you get older you will become more independent. You will also have to take more responsibility for your own safety. You will still be cared for by your parents or carers and teachers, but you will have to make decisions both big and small about how you allow others to treat you.

Taking responsibility for your own safety is exciting and will help you develop confidence and **self-esteem**. Looking **confident** and staying aware of what is happening around you will help keep you safe.

Believe in yourself. Have the courage and confidence to keep yourself and others safe.

4

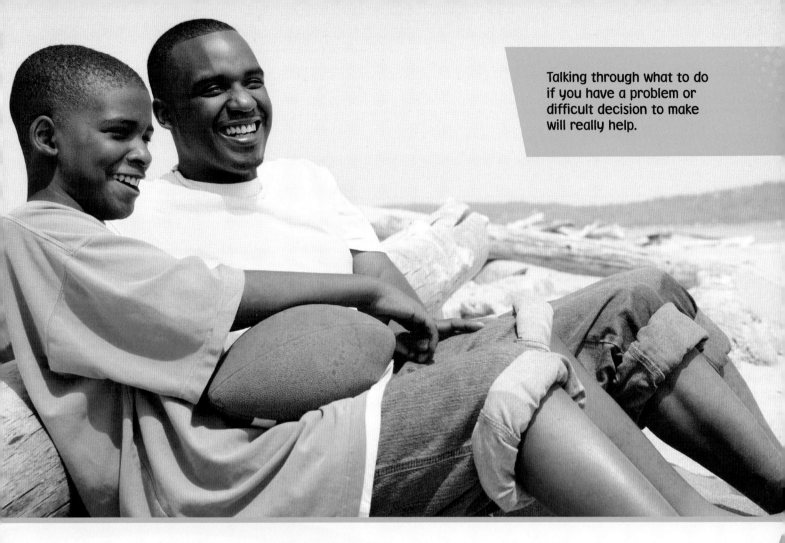

Talking through what to do if you have a problem or difficult decision to make will really help.

Sometimes you will have to think about situations and decide what is the right thing to do. It might be hard to know how to act for the best. If you are unsure, it is a good idea to talk to an adult you trust. You could speak to a parent or carer, a teacher or school counsellor, a family friend, youth leader or religious leader.

SAFETY TIP

If you don't feel able to speak to any adults that you know about a problem, call a helpline. There are some phone numbers on page 32. They won't tell anyone that you have called them.

HELPING OUT

Your family – especially your parents or carers – are responsible for looking after you and keeping you safe. As you grow up, there will be times when you will have to help to look after other members of your family, especially younger brothers and sisters.

Family should be loving, caring and respectful to one another and look out for each other's safety.

You can help your parents keep toddlers safe by watching them when your parents leave the room or when they are busy in the kitchen. If a parent asks you to look after a very young child, you should not leave them alone, even for a minute – accidents can happen very quickly.

SAFETY TIP

Make sure you shut baby gates, and remove any objects left on the stairs. Close windows and doors so younger children can't get out or hurt themselves.

You will seem very grown-up to a young child. They may want to copy what you do. So be careful not to do anything that might cause an accident if they try to do the same. Remember that very young children tend to put things in their mouths. Keep harmful things, such as nail varnish remover or glue, out of reach with the caps on tight.

Helping to look after younger members of the family benefits the whole family, including you.

EMERGENCY!

It is unlikely you will ever need to contact the emergency services. But if there is an emergency and there is no adult around, you will need to take charge of the situation. An emergency is when there is a fire or a serious accident and people are hurt or in danger.

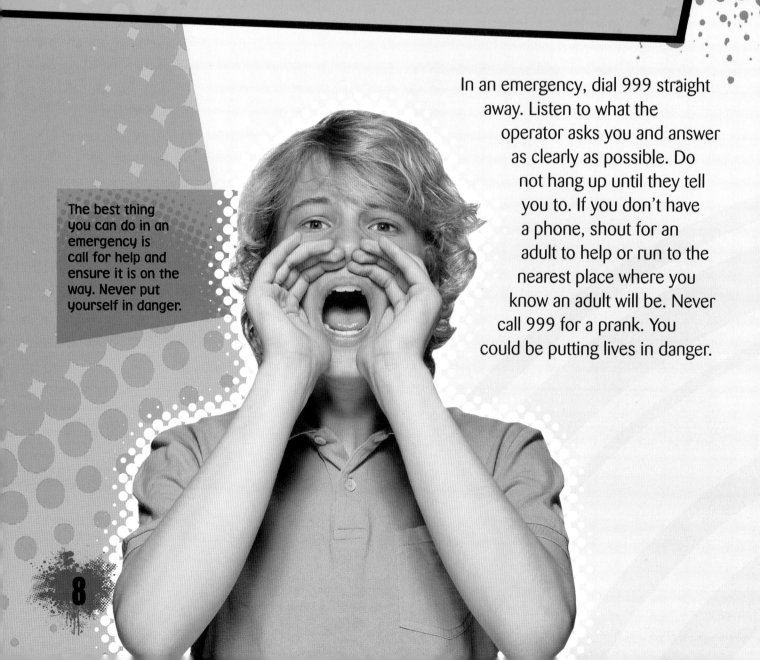

The best thing you can do in an emergency is call for help and ensure it is on the way. Never put yourself in danger.

In an emergency, dial 999 straight away. Listen to what the operator asks you and answer as clearly as possible. Do not hang up until they tell you to. If you don't have a phone, shout for an adult to help or run to the nearest place where you know an adult will be. Never call 999 for a prank. You could be putting lives in danger.

SAFETY TIP

It is a good idea to learn some basic first aid. Ask at school or look online to see if there are any courses locally.

If the emergency is an accident and someone is hurt, don't move them as this may make their injury worse. Wait for the ambulance to arrive. If there is a fire and someone is trapped, do not risk your own safety to rescue them.

Any information you have can be valuable to the emergency services, so stay calm and be as clear as you can.

ANGER AND ARGUMENTS

Even in the happiest home, adults can get stressed and become angry. They may behave in a scary or unpredictable way. If they are especially upset, they may even throw things or lash out. If this happens, the best thing to do is to quietly leave the room.

Sometimes, adults who are stressed or unhappy start to shout and behave in an **aggressive** way. It might happen after they have been drinking alcohol. This can be frightening. When they are calm again, tell them how their shouting or fighting made you feel. If it happens again, talk to an adult you trust. If you ever feel you are in danger, you can call the police at any time of the day or night.

Parents fighting can be frightening. Don't try to stop a fight or you might get hurt by accident.

If a parent has hurt you or a brother or sister, and you don't know who to talk to, call a helpline. Someone who cares will be waiting to listen to you.

Some parents might discipline their children with a smack. However, it is never right for anyone to hit another person so hard that it causes bruises or swelling or leaves a mark. If you, or another member of your family, are being hit or physically hurt by someone you should tell a person you trust straight away.

Talking to someone can help you to cope with what is happening and make it less scary.

11

FAMILY MATTERS

As you get older, you will want to take responsibility for your own safety, and that's good. But your parents have a legal duty to look after you until you are 16. This means keeping you safe, feeding you properly and making sure you are clean. They must also ensure you get a good night's sleep and go to school.

If a parent or carer doesn't do all of these things they could be **neglecting** you. This can happen for lots of different reasons. Maybe a parent is suffering from **alcoholism** (drinking too much) or **depression**, or just can't cope. Don't be embarrassed to ask a teacher or trusted adult for help. The sooner you do, the better it will be for the whole family.

Most families enjoy being together and taking care of each other.

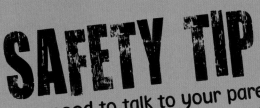

SAFETY TIP

If you need to talk to your parents about a problem, choose a quiet time so you can talk without interruption, such as a car journey or a mealtime.

Families can change and new people may come to live in your home. If there are any problems, such as being bullied by a new member of the family, try to talk to a parent about it. Starting over as a new family is hard for everyone, but no one has to put up with physical or **verbal abuse** just to keep a parent happy.

It might not be easy to speak up, but if your parent or carer doesn't know what's going on, they can't do anything about it.

PET SAFETY

Most family pets are well behaved and enjoy playing and being with people, but not all pets are the same. Even the most friendly pet could suddenly bite if it is feeling scared or is hurt or is unsure about strangers. Pets are not toys so be gentle and careful with them.

Remember that your pet trusts you. You should respect your pet and be kind to it.

Most animals are very protective of their food. Never tease animals with food or try to play with them when they are eating. They won't understand it is a game and might get angry or confused and snap. After giving your pet its bowl, leave it alone to eat its food.

SAFETY TIP

If you come across a dog on its own, don't touch it. If you are concerned about it, tell a trusted adult such as a police officer.

No matter how much of an animal-lover you are, you still need to take extra care around friends' dogs. Even if a dog knows you well, it won't see you as part of its 'pack' or family. Never play-fight with a friend in front of their dog – the dog may be confused and try to protect them.

Family pets usually enjoy being around young people and love to be stroked, but always ask the owner first.

PEER PRESSURE

Your friends are a very important part of your life, and you won't want to fall out with them. But what if they try to persuade you to do things that are dangerous? It can be very difficult to say 'no' to people who you want to like you. This is called peer pressure.

Having friends is a good thing – they are fun to hang out with, and will help you cope with bad times. However, sometimes friends might try to make you do things you know are unsafe. They might dare you to run across a railway track or encourage you to try cigarettes, alcohol or drugs.

True friends are special. They understand and care about one another. They look out for each other.

You may feel that you have to go along with what your friends say because otherwise they will lose respect for you, or think you are 'chicken'. This kind of peer pressure is upsetting but you should still stand up for what you think is right. Real friends will respect your views. The truth is that no one admires someone who lets themselves be pushed around.

If your friends tease you, you have the right to leave. Call a parent for advice or to come and get you.

SAFETY AT HOME

Home is the place where you will feel most safe and relaxed. That said, it's a good idea to be aware of some possible dangers around the house. By being responsible and following a few basic rules, you can make sure that you and your family are safe.

Always put leftover food in the fridge. Don't eat anything that has been left out overnight – it could make you ill.

Always be careful in the kitchen. It's not a good idea to run or play roughly around someone who is cooking – a small bump could cause them to spill boiling water or slip with a knife. Never use sharp knives, electrical equipment, ovens or microwaves without permission from an adult. And remember that it is dangerous to put anything made of metal into a toaster.

SAFETY TIP

If you are at home without any adults, don't answer the door. If someone you don't know phones, say your parents are busy and can't come to the phone. Don't say they are out.

It's important to be aware of fire hazards. Never use matches or candles unless you are with adults. You could cause a fire, and dripping candle wax can hurt if you get it on your hands. If you have been given scented candles, save them for when an adult is around. Remember not to cover lamps with fabric. A strong bulb could cause them to burn.

If there is a fire in the house, you should tell an adult straight away. Do not try to put a fire out yourself.

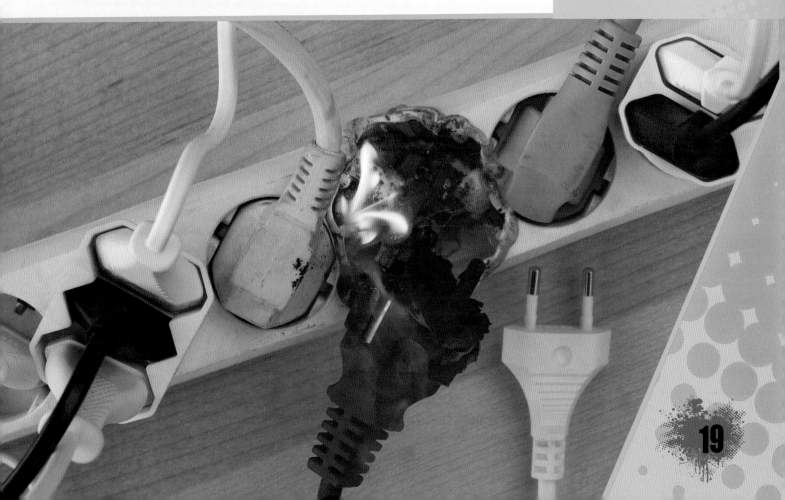

OUT WITH FRIENDS

When you are out and about with adults, it's easy to rely on them to steer you clear of dangers. When you're out with friends, you need to use your own instincts and common sense. You still need to take care when crossing the road and avoid unsafe places.

Being out with friends is fun, but to stay safe you need to be prepared. Think about what would happen if you became separated. Arrange a meeting place in case one of you gets lost, and make sure you know a parent's phone number – even if you own a mobile, you can't always rely on it.

You can have great fun with friends if you stay aware and look out for one another.

SAFETY TIP

Keep some money for emergencies. Put the money in a separate pocket or purse so you don't spend it by mistake.

If you're out with friends shopping or catching up on the gossip, keep valuables safely tucked away from sight in a bag or pocket and keep your belongings close to you. **Pickpockets** can move quickly to snatch a bag or purse if they think you are distracted chatting with friends.

Keep your purse, mobile, coat and other valuables within eyesight and close to you when you're in a café or restaurant.

GOING TO FRIENDS' HOUSES

It's great to visit a friend for tea or to stay over. Being out without parents or carers is exciting but it means you have to take responsibility for your own safety. Give your parents the full address and telephone number of where you'll be, and let them know if your plans change. They'll be impressed by how responsible you are.

Different families have different rules. When you are invited to a new friend's house, you should do your best to fit in with their routines. However, remember that your own family's rules are important, too. Don't do anything there that you wouldn't be allowed to do at home, even if your friend or their parents say it's okay.

Packing for a sleepover is fun but, in the excitement, don't forget any medicines you need to take or your inhaler.

SAFETY TIP

If you have a mobile phone, make sure it is topped up. Remember to charge it, too, so you can always call home if you need to.

If you are ever at a friend's house and feel unsafe for any reason, say you don't feel well and call a parent or carer to come and collect you. Don't think you are being silly – trust your instincts. It's natural to worry about your friend's feelings, but your own safety is more important.

Don't go out in a neighbourhood you don't know after dark, unless you have an adult with you.

YOUR BODY BELONGS TO YOU

You are in charge of your body, and what happens to your body should always be your choice. When it comes to your body, no one else has the right to do – or make you do – anything that feels wrong or scares you. Not even people who you love or who love you have that right.

It is great to be hugged, to hold hands, and to be physically close to people you love and trust. Good touching can make you feel safe, calm you down when you are angry, and comfort you when you are upset. But bad touching can make you feel scared and unhappy. Bad touching is in places that are private and it is wrong.

A big hug from someone close makes you feel safe and loved.

24

SAFETY TIP

If you feel too embarrassed to talk to a trusted adult about someone touching you, phone a helpline for advice.

No one should ask to look at or touch your private parts; the bits of your body covered by underwear, such as pants and a bra. So learn the **PANTS** rule –

Privates are private!

Always remember your body belongs to you.

No means no.

Talk about secrets that upset you.

Speak up – someone can help.

if someone asks to take pictures of you, or asks you to take pictures of yourself, and it feels bad or wrong – then say 'no' and tell someone you trust.

GOOD SECRETS AND BAD SECRETS

Good secrets, such as what you are buying someone for Christmas or a surprise party, are great fun and you can share these with people you love and trust. Bad secrets are a worry and are not secrets you want to keep.

When someone does something wrong, they might not want others to know. They might tell you to keep it a secret. They could even say that people won't believe you if you tell the truth, or that it is your fault. Ignore what they say. No adult should ask you to keep secrets from your parents or carers. What they are asking you to do is wrong – so don't listen.

If someone tells you to keep a bad secret be strong, stand up for yourself and tell someone. It will make you feel much better.

SAFETY TIP

If the person asking you to keep secrets is a family friend, make sure you are never alone with that person. Always keep close to someone you trust until you get things sorted out.

If an adult gives a young person secret presents or wants them to keep meetings and conversations secret, it is likely that they are trying to gain the young person's trust for bad reasons. They might not be as friendly and nice as they seem to be. If this is happening to you or a friend of yours, you must tell your parents or an adult you trust.

If your parents don't believe you for any reason, don't give up. You need to be heard. Phone a helpline or talk to another trusted adult.

SUMMARIZER

Here's a reminder of the most important points made in the book. Look back if you want to see more information about anything.

1 As you grow up, you will need to take more responsibility for your own safety.

2 Remember basic safety rules at home, especially in the kitchen. Be aware of dangers to younger brothers and sisters.

3 In an emergency, dial 999 straight away. Don't risk your own safety.

4 Every family has arguments. However, if you are worried you should speak to a trusted adult.

5 Don't eat anything that might make you ill. If in doubt, don't eat it.

6 Never tease a dog with food – not even one that you know well. Be mindful of its natural instincts to protect its owners and its home.

7 When out with friends, stay aware of what is happening around you and keep your valuables safe.

8 Don't let friends put pressure on you to do things you don't want to do. Stand up for what you believe to be right.

9 When visiting a friend's house, you have to take responsibility for your own safety. Let your parents or carers know where you are.

10 Remember the **PANTS** rule:

Privates are private!
Always remember your body belongs to you.
No means no.
Talk about secrets that upset you.
Speak up – someone can help.

11 If someone asks you to keep a bad secret, one that makes you unhappy, you must tell an adult you trust.

GLOSSARY

abuse unfair, cruel or violent treatment of someone

aggressive violent or threatening

alcoholism being dependent on alcohol; having an uncontrollable need to drink alcohol

confident believing that you can do something well and succeed

depression when a person feels very sad and hopeless

hazards dangers

helpline a telephone service that provides advice and information about problems

independent able to do things without the help of another person

instincts feelings you may have about a person, a place or a situation that you can't explain. Sometimes your instincts may tell you when a person is good or bad.

legal duty something that a person must do by law

neglecting when parents or carers do not look after their children

peer pressure when friends or classmates try to make you do something you don't want to do

peers people of the same age, group or class

pickpockets criminals who steal purses, bags and other small personal valuables by taking them when someone isn't looking

responsibility the job of taking care of something in the right way

self-esteem positive feeling about yourself and your worth

siblings brothers and sisters

unpredictable things that happen unexpectedly and that are not normal

verbal something that is spoken

FURTHER INFORMATION

Websites

www.childline.org.uk
The Childline website has advice and information on all sorts of issues relating to family and friends.

www.juniorcitizen.org.uk
Games and graphics for instant info on how to stay safe around the house and when out and about.

www.kidshealth.org
Information on many of the issues covered in this book

www.nspcc.org.uk
Lots of practical help and advice and more info on the PANTS rule.

Books

Bullies, Bigmouths and So-Called Friends, **Jenny Alexander**, Hodder Children's Books, 2006
Divorce and Separation, **Patricia J. Murphy**, Heinemann First Library, 2008
Peer Pressure, **Elizabeth Raum**, Heinemann First Library, 2009
Safety Around the House, **Ana Deboo**, Heinemann First Library, 2008

Helplines

(UK) Childline 0800 1111
Childline is a helpline for young people who need to talk about problems.

(Australia) Kids' Helpline 1800 55 1800
Free phone or online counselling with a personal counsellor. www.kidshelp.com.au/teens/get-help/web-counselling/

(UK) Samaritans 08457 90 90 90
A telephone helpline run by volunteers who are there to listen to your problems and help you with your feelings.

INDEX

SERIES CONTENTS

Keeping Safe around Alcohol, Drugs and Cigarettes
- Avoiding Harm from Drink, Drugs and Cigarettes
- Being Around Drink, Drugs and Cigarettes
- About Alcohol • Alcohol Around You • Alcohol and You
- Cigarettes and Addiction • Dangers of Smoking
- Avoiding Smoke • About Drugs • Dangers of Drug Misuse
- Dangers to You • Taking a Stand

Keeping Safe on the Street
- Be Street Smart • Know Your Journey
- Stay Aware • Dog Dangers • Stranger Danger
- Trouble on the Streets • Safe Cycling
- Safe Skateboarding • Keep Away from Building Sites
- Keep Away from Rail Tracks
- Stay Safe on Public Transport • After Dark

Keeping Safe Online
- Having a Happy Online Life • Cyberbullying
- Using Social Media Safely • Share Carefully
- Keep Your Information Safe • Online Chat
- Stay in Your Comfort Zone • Too Much
- Click With Care • Going Viral • Infected Computer
- Dealing With Problems

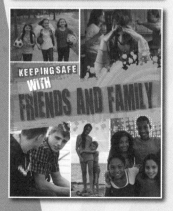

Keeping Safe with Friends and Family
- Making Decisions • Helping Out • Emergency!
- Anger and Arguments • Family Matters • Pet Safety
- Peer Pressure • Safety at Home • Out with Friends
- Going to Friends' Houses • Your Body Belongs to You
- Good Secrets and Bad Secrets